This book is about President and Mrs. Woodrow Wilson and

How the

SHEEP

Helped Win the War

Edith Bolling Wilson Birthplace Foundation and Museum

www.mascotbooks.com

How the SHEEP Helped Win the War

Cover, book design, and illustrations by Andrew Beaver
Cover photo: Library of Congress
Interior photos: Library of Congress
Edith Bolling Wilson, My Memoir

For more information, please contact:
Mascot Books
560 Herndon Parkway #120
Herndon, VA 20170
info@mascotbooks.com

Edith Bolling Wilson Birthplace Foundation and Museum
145 E. Main Street
Wytheville, VA 24382
www.edithbollingwilson.org

Library of Congress Control Number: 2016911168

CPSIA Code: PRT1016A
ISBN: 978-1-63177-889-6

Printed in the United States

This book is dedicated to the many friends of the
Edith Bolling Wilson Birthplace Foundation and Museum
who gave of their time and talents to bring
How the SHEEP Helped Win the War
to its first publication.

Have you ever met a sheep who could read and talk? Well, now you have! My name is Woolie Wythe and I am the great-grandson of a sheep who lived in the year 1915. I want to tell you how sheep like me helped win the **war**—World War I. First, let me introduce **President Woodrow Wilson** and **First Lady Mrs. Edith Bolling Wilson**.

Woodrow Wilson was **President** of the United States from 1913 to 1921. President Woodrow Wilson and his wife, Edith Bolling Wilson, lived in the **White House** in Washington, D.C.

This picture is of **First Lady** Mrs. Wilson. The wife of the President of the United States is called "First Lady."

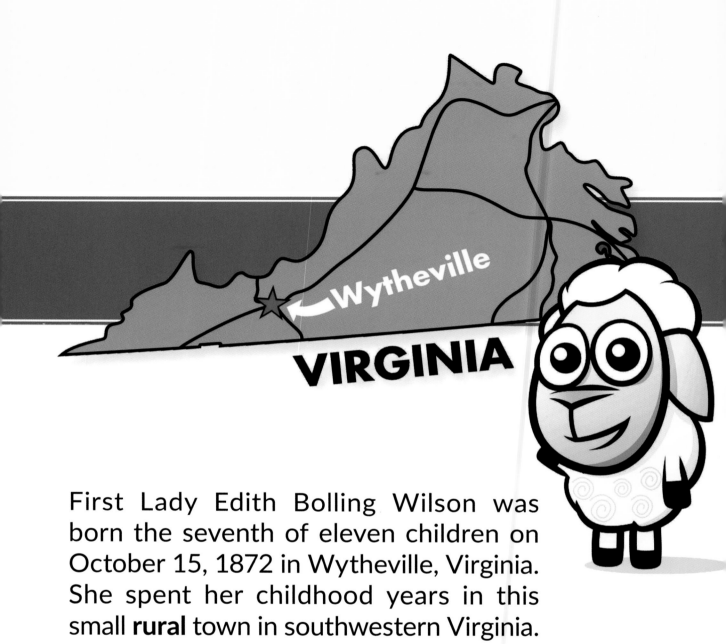

First Lady Edith Bolling Wilson was born the seventh of eleven children on October 15, 1872 in Wytheville, Virginia. She spent her childhood years in this small **rural** town in southwestern Virginia.

What was life like in Wytheville? Life was centered on farming, and many farmers raised sheep for their wool.

This is a picture of Edith at age three.

Edith, schooled at home as a little girl, later experienced two years of formal education away from home. Her family considered education important. Grandmother Bolling taught Edith to knit, crochet, and sew. This knowledge would be helpful when she married the president and became the First Lady in 1915.

World War I began in 1914. The United States joined the fight in 1917. President and Mrs. Wilson set an example of how Americans could **support** the war effort. How did they do that?

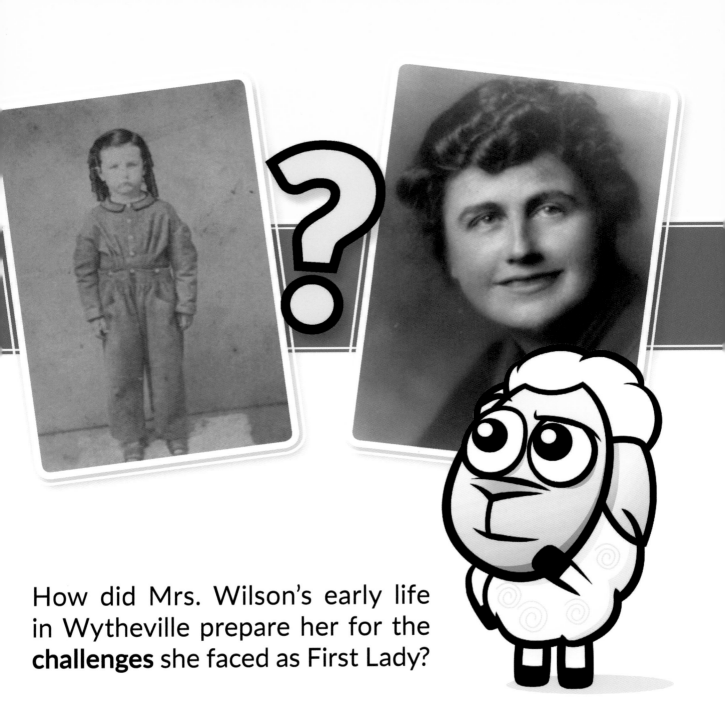

How did Mrs. Wilson's early life in Wytheville prepare her for the **challenges** she faced as First Lady?

During the war, soldiers did not have enough clothing. That was a problem.

When she moved to the White House, Mrs. Wilson brought her sewing machine. She sewed pajamas, shirts, and other items for the Red Cross. The **Red Cross** gave these items to the soldiers.

What did the sheep do to help the soldiers?

How did the sheep help win the war?

It started when President and Mrs. Wilson brought a **flock** of sheep to the White House.

The lambs **frolicked** and played on the White House **lawn** while the sheep **grazed** on the sweet grasses and grew thick coats of wool.

By grazing on the White House lawn, the sheep kept the grass from growing too high. They were the president's lawn mowers!

That was the first good reason
to keep sheep on the
White House lawn!

Since the sheep munched the grass keeping it short, the White House gardeners worked on other wartime duties.

That was the second good reason
to keep sheep on the
White House lawn!

The staff **sheared** the flock's heavy **fleece** coats on the White House lawn.

Can you see the big pile of wool in the picture?

16

The Red Cross auctioned the wool to make money. People called the wool "White House Wool."

How much money did the Red Cross make auctioning the wool?

The White House Wool raised nearly one hundred thousand dollars to help win the war.

Baa, what a lot of money!

That was the third good reason
to keep sheep on the
White House lawn!

The sheep showed the whole world how Americans (and sheep) supported our troops. Now, **YOU** know, too!

And that is...

How the **SHEEP** helped win the war.

Glossary

C

Challenges: Things that are difficult or hard; problems

E

Edith Bolling Wilson: The second wife of U.S. President Woodrow Wilson

F

First Lady: A title used for the wife of the President of the United States

Fleece: The coat or wool that covers a sheep

Flock: A group of animals, such as sheep, goats, or birds that live, travel, or feed together

Frolicked: To play and move about happily

G

Graze: To eat small portions

L

Lawn: A grassy area, such as a yard

P

President: The chief officer elected to preside over the United States of America

R

Rural: Referring to the country or an agricultural area

Red Cross: An organization that provides care for the sick and wounded during disasters

S

Shear: To remove (fleece or hair) by cutting or clipping

Support: Help with a task or giving money

W

War: Fighting or conflict between states or nations

White House: The home of the President of the United States

Woodrow Wilson: The 28th President of the United States from 1913 to 1921

Fun Facts About Edith Bolling Wilson During World War I

Europe: When President and Mrs. Wilson first married in 1915, World War I was raging in Europe.

Adviser: Mrs. Wilson became the President's confidante and trusted adviser. The President valued her opinion and he discussed important matters with her.

First Lady: Mrs. Wilson was the first First Lady to travel with a president to Europe. She attended the Paris Peace Conference. Her presence among the queens and other women royalty of Europe put the position of First Lady on an equivalent standing helping to define the American role of First Lady in an international context.

Technology: Mrs. Wilson embraced technology of the time during the war. The President taught Mrs. Wilson a secret wartime code. She helped the war effort by learning to code and decode war messages.

Patriotic Efforts: Mrs. Wilson embraced the patriotic efforts to save resources for the war effort by wearing thrift clothing. She limited the White House use of meat, wheat, and gasoline.

Pocahontas: Edith Bolling Wilson was a direct descendant of Pocahontas. Pocahontas was a Native American known for her association with colonial settlers during their first years in Jamestown, Virginia.

Volunteer: Mrs. Wilson volunteered at the American Red Cross canteen at Union

Station in Washington, D.C. This is where soldiers stopped for a meal while traveling to or from war.

Woodrow Wilson: Reading was a struggle for young Woodrow. He was ten years old when he learned to read. Through his own determination and self-discipline he overcame these difficulties, becoming the most educated of all presidents.

World Peace: Mrs. Wilson supported the President's League of Nations and throughout her life promoted his vision for world peace.

Edith Bolling, age thirteen

Acknowledgments

I once read the words, **"Ideas don't work if you don't."**

A friend from a local preschool in our town of Wytheville approached the museum about presenting a program related to Edith Bolling Wilson for her young students. An idea was born!

Sheep on The White House Lawn was the program idea for the young boys and girls learning about the role sheep played during a critical time in our nation's history. The story of President and Mrs. Wilson placing a flock of sheep to graze on the lawn of the White House during World War I demonstrated how the Wilsons' frugal upbringings influenced life at the White House. With time, that decision had a big impact on supporting the war effort and setting an example of conservation for the country. From that idea for the school program, a book telling the story through the voice of a sheep was born.

I would like to recognize my sister Joyce Covey for co-authoring the book with me. A schoolteacher with over thirty-five years of experience, she gave voice to the sheep and dedicated her time and talents to make the book both educational and fun. This book would not be possible without her participation.

Together, Joyce and I wish to thank the many friends of the museum for their contributions of time, expertise, and insight in creating this book. The illustrations and initial style of the book were designed by Andrew Beavers. Hours of editing were contributed by Deborah Kemper, a member of the Museum's Board of Trustees. Cary Fuller, great-nephew of Mrs. Wilson, reviewed the book and offered suggestions. Pam Newberry and Julie Newberry aided the process that completed the book's format. Sherri Case, a member of the Museum's Board of Trustees, offered support and kept the museum office running smoothly while research was conducted.

To the many others, too numerous to mention, thank you for your input and suggestions. To the dedicated Board of Trustees for the Edith Bolling Wilson Birthplace Foundation, thank you for your encouragement not only for this book but also for your vision for the museum and Bolling Home to honor First Lady Mrs. Wilson. Last, but not least, a special thank you to my husband Bill for his dedication and commitment to preserving First Lady Mrs. Wilson's birthplace and childhood home—and for his love and support of my little idea to write a book about sheep on the White House lawn.

About the Authors

Joyce Covey's journey to co-author **How the SHEEP Helped Win the War** began with a desire to provide young students a visual to improve their understanding of a World War I history concept that she taught as an elementary school teacher. Joyce is a graduate of Radford College and a long serving member of Alpha Delta Kappa, an international honorary sorority for women educators.

A retired teacher with over thirty-five years of teaching experience, Joyce resides in Pulaski, Virginia, with her husband M.G. She hopes that young readers will find this book enjoyable and perhaps excite the budding history scholar!

As founder of the Edith Bolling Wilson Birthplace Foundation, Farron Smith is dedicated to preserving the only birthplace home museum of a First Lady in Virginia. After graduating from Radford College, she and her husband Bill moved to Wytheville, Virginia, where her career path has taken many different roads.

Farron is most proud of her contributions sharing the story of a little girl from Wytheville, Virginia, who grew up to become First Lady of the United States. **How the SHEEP Helped Win the War** is informative, educational, and will spark the imagination of children of all ages—adults will love it too!

Thank You to Our Sponsors

 BOLLING WILSON HOTEL
AT WYTHEVILLE

GRAZE
ON MAIN

 **BB&T**  FARM CREDIT  CAMRETT LOGISTICS

 Serta  GRAND Home Furnishings

FIRST SENTINEL BANK

National Bank

First Community Bank

Bank of Floyd, a Division of Grayson National Bank

First Bank & Trust Company

BANKERS INSURANCE George James, CIC

WYTHEVILLE MOOSE LODGE 394

Mr. Ron Sharrock

Dr. and Mrs. Dean Sprinkle